GUIDE FOR TEACHERS

Duncan Shiels
Hilderstone Adult Education Centre
Broadstairs

Nicole Church
Producer

Contents

A BBC second-stage radio course in French to
follow *A vous la France!*
First broadcast from September 1985

The course consists of:
15 radio programmes
One course book covering the 15 programmes
A set of 3 cassettes
A guide for teachers

Diagrams by John Gilkes

Published to accompany a series of programmes in consultation
with the BBC Continuing Education Advisory Council

Published by BBC Books.
a division of BBC Enterprises Ltd.
80 Wood Lane, London W12 0TT
ISBN 0 563 21148 2

Printed and bound in Great Britain by
Ebenezer Baylis and Son Ltd, Worcester.
Cover printed by Clays Ltd, St Ives, plc

Introduction

The materials
France Extra! is a second stage BBC Radio Self-study Course for
adults, consisting of 15 radio programmes, a course book and three
cassettes.

The radio programmes are to be broadcast from September
1985 to February 1986 at the following times:

On Sunday at 5.00pm to 5.30pm;
repeated on Saturday at 3.30pm to 4.00pm.

The course book is divided into 15 units based around themes
corresponding to the 15 radio programmes.

Each chapter contains:

1 transcripts of interviews and conversations featured on the radio
programme with relevant vocabulary, **Phrases clé** and
comprehension exercises **Avez-vous bien compris?**;

2 **Pour en savoir plus** – an explanatory grammatical section,
including short exercises **Essayez donc!** for immediate checking on
whether a grammar point has been understood;

3 **Le mot juste** – a section on certain words which present difficulty
in usage, particularly the notorious **Faux amis**;

4 **Activités** – exercises designed to reinforce points learnt in the
unit;

5 **A l'écoute** – an exercise in extensive listening (listening for gist),
whereby students are given a task to fulfil by listening to a longer
piece of discourse. There is no transcript;

6 **Faits divers** – listening for pleasure. A short general-interest
documentary with a written introduction. Again there is no
transcript.

Some chapters also contain a **Prononciation** section, giving
guidance on the trickier aspects of French pronunciation and **Le
saviez-vous?** – a background reading passage.

Solutions to **Essayez donc!**, **Activités** and **A l'écoute** appear in
the blue section at the back of the book, along with an index of
grammatical and functional exponents.

The three accompanying cassettes contain most of the recorded
material, including the **A l'écoute** and **Faits divers** pieces which
will not be broadcast in the radio programmes, pronunciation
exercises and gap-filling exercises to give the user an opportunity
to get his/her mouth round new structures.

So what's new about *France Extra*?

Well, one will notice immediately the large amount of authentic *actuality* material. This comes from the belief that it is simply not enough to train people to make utterances in a more or less correct form. Language is more than just expressing things. It is also about processing both written and, more importantly, spoken data. Developing listening skills through exposure to 'real' French is a source of controversy amongst language teachers. How do we give students the necessary exposure to authentic recorded texts without undermining their already fragile confidence?

The answer lies in the demands we make of our students; we need to condition them into accepting and dealing with not being able to understand everything they hear.

The **A l'écoute** and **Faits divers** sections are an attempt to grasp this nettle. They are designed for a student to work at alone, with a cassette, *at his own pace* and it has to be said at this stage that any user of **France Extra!** without access to the cassette between radio programmes or language classes will be at a considerable disadvantage.

Each unit is built around a theme under which several linguistic functions are predicted. Structures are dealt with within the context in which they occur, never in isolation. The learning process is thus cyclical with certain structures occurring in several chapters under different themes and functions. For example, the imperfect tense appears in Chapter Four, *Biographies* under *describing past habits*, in Chapter Seven *Que de Changements dans la vie* . . . within the function *contrasting past and present*, and in Chapter Ten *Du Côté des Femmes* under *recounting background events*.

So why does **France Extra!** have these two main features: lots of listening to unscripted authentic discourse and a cyclical approach to grammar? Quite simply, it is an attempt to create the conditions we all agree are best for learning a foreign language, i.e. those met with when living in the country itself – something all but a tiny few of our students would only dream of being able to do.

For what level of student is *France Extra!* designed?

Ideally a student entering at this stage will have completed the BBC stage one French course **A Vous La France!**. However, it is recognised that many users of **France Extra!** will either not have completed **A Vous La France!** or have already acquired a basic knowledge of French elsewhere.

Here is a loose description, therefore, of what a potential user of **France Extra!** should already be able to do:

1 In communicative terms he/she should be able to operate in the following situations:

  1 introducing oneself and one's background, and asking basic personal information, for example, job, native town/country, family, etc;

  2 buying, hiring and ordering things;

3 asking for and understanding public information, for example, *au Syndicat d'Initiative, au restaurant, à la gare*;

4 using public transport;

5 staying in a hotel;

6 giving and following simple instructions, for example, direction-finding, simple recipes;

7 expressing likes and dislikes;

8 referring to the future;

9 referring to the past.

2 Grammatically he/she should be 'comfortable'
  1 in the present tense of all common verbs;

  2 with the future tense as expressed with *je vais faire* – though he/she will *not* be familiar with the form *je ferai*;

  3 with some verbs used in conjunction with infinitives, for example,
  il faut
  on peut $\Big|$ + *infinitive*
  j'aime

  4 with numbers up to 100, telling the time, dates, days and months.

3 He/she should be *familiar* with, though not wholly competent in the use of, the perfect and imperfect tenses.

In the classroom
Treating adults as adults

The vast majority of language courses based on BBC radio and television series are organised by LEA Adult Education Centres around Britain. At any one time there are around two million adults enrolled at these centres, of which around 300,000 will be studying a foreign language. Well over a third of these choose French. Who are they and why do they come?

According to surveys carried out by the National Institute of Adult and Continuing Education they are characterised by the following:

1 they come mainly from socio-economic groups C1 to C3, especially C3, ie they are predominantly middle class;

2 they are of all ages from 17 to beyond retirement age (there is a proportionately large number of retired people, particularly in day classes);

3 two thirds have previously had some kind of post-school education;

4 they are very motivated to learn and usually have specific reasons for doing so, although these reasons may not always be related directly to the course itself. In the case of language classes there are obviously those who intend to travel to the

country on holiday or on business, but many come to be part of the shared experience of learning in a group, or 'to keep the mind active'. Indeed, in the NIAE survey of 1970 over 40% of students interviewed declared 'self-development' to be their main motive;

5 they are easily discouraged, particularly in language classes. There are two reasons for this: firstly they are often under the mistaken impression that as adults they have somehow 'missed the boat' of language learning. This view, fashionable around the end of the sixties (and based on Lenneberg's 'Critical Age Theory') has been considerably discredited by most research since. *Under the same conditions*, in all areas except that of pronunciation, adults are every bit as good, if not better than children at learning languages. The other reason for adults being so easily discouraged is their often unhappy memories of previous attempts to learn a foreign language, especially at school – hopeless efforts at learning lists of verbs and grammatical rules by heart without ever being given the opportunity to communicate in the language;

6 over 60% of all adult language learners do not attend classes for longer than a year, often dropping out after only one term. There is therefore no shortage of people willing to *try* a language class. This higher-than-average drop-out rate is a source of considerable controversy. Is it an inevitable fact of life related to (5) above? Should language courses be shorter and more intensive, thereby encouraging students to achieve more in a shorter time? Can the way a teacher handles his class influence a student's decision to give up?

I think the answer to all three questions is 'yes'. But while the second question is out of the teacher's immediate domain, the first and third are definitely not. Indeed they are linked. The teacher has an enormous influence over how discouraging or enjoyable an adult's 'return to study' will be.

The social aspect of the class is crucial to this feeling of enjoyment. The content of a course is rarely enough in itself to keep someone coming out on cold and rainy nights. There has to be something else – an interest in the other members of the class, a feeling of belonging – the idea that even if you, the teacher, were not there the group would still want to come and meet together.

How do we promote this atmosphere? The following tips might help:

1 Learn everyone's name and encourage them to do the same (see **The first class**).

2 Do not dominate. Let group members take initiatives in talking to each other.

3 Encourage a regular exchange of views on how the course is going, what people think and feel about the often frustrating process.

4 Encourage the group to use the bar or café facilities after the class.

5 Encourage contact outside the class – giving each other lifts, sharing cassettes.

6 If someone is absent find out why, inform the others and keep in touch with the person until he/she returns – assuming he/she intends to do so.

But what of this mysterious process by which adults learn a language? What is the best way to go about teaching a group of mixed personalities, high on motivation and low on confidence?

At this point let us examine some very important ideas currently circulating in the world of English as a Foreign Language. So far, I have used the phrase 'learning a language' loosely. It is now generally accepted that there are two processes at work: *conscious learning* and *acquisition*.

Ideas based around this distinction between language learning and language acquisition have been formulated and promoted by, among others, Stephen Krashen of the University of Southern California, in his Monitor Theory (see **Book List**) and are worthy of a brief mention here.

Language acquisition is very similar to the process by which children acquire first and second languages. It requires meaningful interaction in the target language – natural communication – in which speakers are concerned not with the form of their utterances but with the messages they are conveying and understanding. There is no error correction and no teaching of rules. According to their understanding of the *message* the *acquirer* will self-correct on the basis of a *feel for grammaticalness*.

Conscious language learning, on the other hand, depends on both the presentation of explicit rules and error correction. It corresponds to how most of us have approached the teaching of languages in the past.

Krashen's Monitor Theory suggests that conscious learning serves only as a *monitor* of linguistic performance. In general our fluency is based on our acquired body of language, on what we have picked up through active communication.

I would suggest here that in the past we have concentrated almost entirely on language *learning* as a means to mastery of the target language at the expense of creating opportunities for language acquisition to take place. This might explain why results have been so poor and why the attitudes described in (6) above have prevailed. So what are the conditions necessary for adults to *acquire* or pick up language?

Krashen gives three conditions:

1 Comprehensible Input – acquisition takes place when the student understands messages expressed in the target language.

2 A stress-free environment – a relaxed state of mind 'lets in' far more comprehensible input than a stressed one.

3 The right to be silent – the acquirer chooses his moment to speak, no-one else.

Recognition of both the right to choose how one operates in the target language and the student's need to understand input is fundamental to treating adults as adults. Might it not also be the key to better results?

What implications does all this have for such things as deciding how much English is used in class, getting people to practise pronunciation, managing pair and group work, role plays – in short 'getting them talking in French'?

As far as the use of English is concerned, teachers should stick to French but be willing to speak in English at the request of the students. Suggest but *do not* insist that they use French in 'real' communication (For example, 'Tu peux repasser la cassette? Je ne l'ai pas bien saisie.' 'Qu'est-ce qu'il fait chaud dans cette salle!') Under these conditions most people will opt for French, but it must be their choice and they do have a right not to speak at all. By listening they are still acquiring.

When repeating phrases for pronunciation, use choral repetition so that people can 'hide', but still speak if they wish to. Only have individuals speak in front of the others who wish to do so.

When the group is working in pairs or groups, be *available* but avoid *surveillance*. One can monitor students' performance without hovering over them. Let them feel they can call you as they need you. Remember that the teacher's role is essentially that of a resource.

But are there any activities which actually promote meaningful interaction while at the same time recognising this right to choose?

This Guide for Teachers provides two such activities at various points in the course. The first is entirely student-controlled, the second is initiated by the teacher, but then left in the hands of the group.

'Say what you want' sessions

This is an attempt to tap the group's desire to talk to one another socially in the way that is usually happening in English before the teacher arrives.

1 The procedure is as follows:

The group forms a circle of chairs which does not include the teacher. Inside the circle is a tape recorder with, if possible, a separate microphone with an on/off switch. The teacher is outside the circle and available to be referred to. When a member of the group wants to say something, he picks up the microphone and indicates to the teacher what he wants to say in English. The teacher then gives him the translation into French and the student practises it with the teacher until he is ready to record it, either as a complete utterance or in small sections. He then puts the microphone back for someone else to pick up if they want. Whenever someone wants to speak the procedure is the same: pick up the microphone, consult the teacher, practise and record.

If a separate microphone is not available, most cassette recorders have their own microphone and it would then be a question of picking up the recorder and using the pause button with the 'Record' button pressed.

In this way, a more or less fluent conversation is built up on the tape with the group having complete control over what is said, when, and by whom.

2 The next step, again at the initiative of the group, is to listen to the complete conversation without interruption. This invariably gives a feeling of satisfaction of having produced a more or less perfect conversation through the use of the teacher as a resource. Artificial though this satisfaction may be, it is a valuable confidence-builder. Give time here for feedback on how people felt about 'their' conversation.

3 The next very important stage is to write up (on an overhead projector (OHP) transparency for photocopying if possible) the whole conversation, line by line, with the student's name against what he or she has said, exactly as he/she said it. If there are errors of either form or pronunciation these should be indicated at this stage (*never* during the recording or listening). Individuals are free to ask questions at any time. Answer these questions fully, but resist the temptation to answer questions which have *not* been asked by giving grammatical explanations that only you think necessary. In any case, the students will only take on board what is relevant to them.

4 Having written out the transcript, ask the students if there are any words or phrases they would like to practise for pronunciation or for which they would like a translation, then, if you have used a transparency, photocopy the transcript for them to take home. (If you do not have access to an OHP write it out and photocopy it for next time.)

The whole process takes between $1\frac{1}{2}$ and 2 hours. The input is comprehensible, having been initiated in English, the environment is stress-free (once the students have become accustomed to the tape recorder) – indeed, the experience has proved very enjoyable for participants, and individuals maintain their right to be silent. No one speaks unless they want to. You will find that those who do not speak still take an interest in what is said and therefore acquire. The most important feature of these sessions is that they correspond to how one operates in the country itself: one needs to say something and one finds a means of saying it, ideally by consulting someone who speaks both languages. For more information on this approach – called 'Community Language Learning' – see the Reading List.

Simulations

What is a simulation? Leo Jones in his book *Eight Simulations* (see **Book List**) defines it as follows:

'A simulation is a representation of a series of real-life events. The classroom represents the setting where the events take place. The events are accelerated and simplified to fit them into the time available and to ensure the maximum amount of language activity.'

A simulation is different from role play or drama in that the participant is at all times himself/herself and does not have to assume a different personality. The involvement felt by all the participants in the tasks they have to do means that for a couple of hours they are taken beyond the parameters of the 'language class'. Everyone is responsible for his/her own decisions and actions and also shares in any collective decisions taken.

There are no 'right answers' to a simulation. What happens in the end depends on the decisions and actions of the participants. In reaching that end they will be using a variety of language skills while concentrating on their communicative tasks, not on formal accuracy. At least part of the simulations should be recorded for future reference (in certain simulations this will be part of the task anyway). This is as much for the participants as for the teacher. It gives them an opportunity later to monitor themselves both for pronunciation and for accuracy.

The four skills – striking a balance

Reading, writing, listening and speaking have tended in part to be considered as separate elements. However, in real life many activities are a combination of two or more of these skills: listening and speaking; listening, writing and speaking (eg taking a message); reading and speaking (eg finding information for someone) and so on. If we assume that most of our students are learning French with a view to conversing with French people and surviving in a French-speaking country, the balance of skills needed will be weighted towards listening and speaking with the skills of reading and especially writing less frequently called upon. It is important that we bear this strongly in mind when planning our classes. Practice in listening and speaking must be a priority.

All the same, what will our students need to be able to read and write if they should visit a French-speaking country? This is a suggested list:

Reading:	notices	*Writing:*	messages
	brochures		simple letters
	instructions		postcards
	timetables		filling in forms
	forms		
	bills		
	letters and postcards		
	messages		

We must therefore be careful when giving them reading and writing practice that we are giving them exercises which are relevant to these needs. Most of the reading material in **France Extra!** is taken from brochures, notices or sets of instructions. Literary texts are out! Similarly, a composition-type writing task along the lines of 'Pourquoi j'aime l'automne' is not the best use of the student's time.

However, we must consider the importance of reading and writing in the learning process. Adults' ability to retain new language presented to them orally is very limited. Writing things down serves as a vital aide-memoire and so there should always be moments in the lesson when new words or phrases are written up by the teacher for the students to copy down with special attention to spelling. If these opportunities are not given, adults rapidly become frustrated and try to write things down anyway, usually inaccurately, at moments when their attention is required for other activities.

Exploiting taped materials

As was mentioned in the Introduction the dialogues and interviews recorded in France are the most important elements of *France Extra!*. The thinking behind what may seem difficult unscripted material is that this is exactly what our students are going to meet as soon as they set foot on the other side of the Channel. Our job is to prepare them for coping with real discourse and not to protect them from it. We can reduce their fear by, firstly, eliminating the expectation inherent in adults of understanding everything that is said and, secondly, showing that to understand the message they do not need to grasp every single word. This can only be done through their own experience of *achieving* tasks.

Each unit in the Guide for Teachers has advice on exploiting at least one of the transcripted interviews, but here are some general principles which apply to any of the listening materials in *France Extra!*

1 Check the cassette recorder and find the right point on the tape *before* the class begins.

2 Use short pieces of less than a minute for language work. Concentration wanes quickly!

3 Set *fulfillable* tasks. This will build confidence. Tasks which they have no hope of completing, for example detailed questions, the answers to which depend on hearing one barely recognisable word, will most certainly destroy confidence.

4 Set the scene and pre-teach a minimum of key words or phrases so that the first condition of acquisition, *comprehensible input*, is, wherever possible, fulfilled. Students will have little chance of understanding anything if they don't know at least broadly what is going on.

Longer dialogues may still be exploited in class using a technique known as 'jigsaw' listening. You will need three copies of the cassette and three cassette recorders (perhaps two of the students could bring theirs if your centre cannot provide them). Divide the class into three groups and have each group glean different information by listening to different parts of the dialogue. An extra room would be ideal for this part, but, provided the volume is kept low, the three groups can work in three corners of a large room.

The second part of the exercise is to re-mix the groups as in

Figure I so that each member of the second group has heard a different section. The information is then exchanged within these second groups.

Not only is this a listening exercise but is also involves student interaction and combines all four skills.

Step 1
Listening

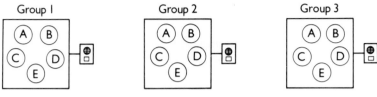

Step 2
Remixed groups
for information
exchange

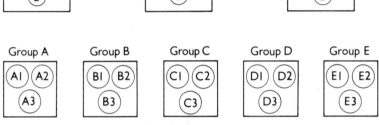

Figure I

As regards the **A l'écoute** and **Faits divers** sections, students should be encouraged to work on the **A l'écoute** sections on their own at home. These are too long for use in their entirety during class time, but parts of them may be referred to when checking whether the students have managed the exercise.

The **Faits divers** sections do not have exercises and are designed to entertain. They provide an opportunity for individuals to do extra listening for pleasure, again in their own time and at their own choice.

Exploiting written materials
The general principles for setting reading tasks are similar to those which apply to listening exercises:

1 Use short pieces in class. The **Le saviez-vous?** sections in *France Extra!* are ideal.

2 Set fulfillable tasks. Design comprehension questions which encourage the student to extract the general 'message' and not get bogged down in detail.

3 Make the context clear. Pre-teach only *key* words or phrases – those which are vital to understanding the general message.

4 Avoid having individuals read aloud. It is wasteful of time and boring for all but one of the group, whilst the benefit to the 'victim' is negligible. There are more efficient ways of dealing with pronunciation outlined below. Leave them to read quietly at their own pace.

5 For longer texts 'jigsaw' reading is ideal. The procedure is the same as for 'jigsaw' listening above with the added bonus that there is no need for either an extra room or any extra equipment.

Encourage people to read outside class and help them to choose appropriate material (for example, the introductory paragraph to **Faits divers**). Encourage individuals to talk, in English if they want, about what they have read.

Pronunciation

Always give students the opportunity to get their mouth round new exponents. This is best done through choral repetition. Make sure they are both watching your mouth and listening to you as you speak the model. Then signal clearly that you want them to repeat and do it several times so that they become aware of the stress and rhythm. It is worth explaining at the outset the difference between French and English stress and intonation patterns. This is very well explained in the **Prononciation** section of Chapter Ten. In fact, all the **Prononciation** sections are worth practising in class. As well as having the class repeat in unison, give people the chance to say it individually if they want to. Let people come forward rather than 'picking on' the unfortunate person who isn't getting it right. He/she will choose his/her moment to ask you. Choral repetition may seem boring to a teacher fluent in French, but students find it both enjoyable and valuable in avoiding later confusion and embarrassment.

There is no doubt that for adults French pronunciation is very hard to get right. Teacher correction doesn't seem to have much effect. There are two principal reasons for this. The first is something we can do little about: as we get older we do lose the ability to imitate new sounds. The second reason is that without hearing oneself it is often difficult to know what one is doing wrong.

Here we can help by encouraging students to record themselves either on their own or in the Say what you want sessions.

The first class

The first session, being vital in setting the right tone for the rest of the course, should be first and foremost an exercise in getting to know one another, establishing a group 'feeling', and together deciding priorities and ways of working. It should contain the following elements:
1 A *brief* introduction by the teacher.
2 An 'ice-breaker' in French to give everyone, including the teacher, an opportunity to learn names.
3 Finding a consensus – what would they like from the course?
4 Something to go home with.

1 Introducing the course

This should be brief and informative. Start with administrative information such as what they should do if they can't come (give them your telephone number?), how to pay if they haven't yet, where the toilets and cafeteria or bar are and some general information about the centre. It might be an idea to take their addresses and telephone numbers by passing round a sheet of paper.

Tell them a *little* about yourself – if your mother tongue is French something about where you come from and how you come to be working in England. If you are British you might tell them how you came to speak French so well(!)

Give them also a little information about **France Extra!** – at what time it is broadcast on the radio, where to get the book and cassettes and also refer them to the introduction in the student's book.

2   The ice-breaker

I am sure most of us already have our own ways of breaking the ice. One good idea is a name chain. One student begins by giving his name and one fact about himself in French. Each student then does the same but also has to remember the names and facts of those who have spoken before. The teacher, of course, is last!

A colleague of mine just brings in a bottle of wine (or two), distributes glasses and asks people to get up and circulate, chatting casually in French, to whoever they come across. Everyone then sits down as a class and discusses what they have found out about one another.

3   Finding a consensus

This, I feel, is very important in an adult education class. Everyone has their own idea of how they would like to go about learning a language and we all too often fail to take this into account.

Try using a set of blank cards. This is the procedure:

1   Distribute three blank cards per person and ask them to write on each card either something they hope they will be doing in class or one of their own ideas on what is the best way to go about learning French.
2   Collect in the cards, shuffle them, add a few of your own and lay them out on the table.
3   Ask them to get up, go to the table and pick up three cards with which they agree (they may pick up their own). They must pick up three cards.
4   In pairs they reduce their six cards to three.
5   In groups of four they again reduce six cards to the three most important.
6   In groups of between six and eight they put the cards aside and attempt to come to a consensus on the three most important ideas. They then agree on a spokesman to report back on their discussion to the rest of the class.
7   The class comes back together to listen to each spokesman.

Why, you may ask, doesn't the teacher simply ask them what their expectations are as a class?

Not everyone is prepared to speak in front of the others and so you are not likely to get a very accurate idea of the expectations and approach of the group as a whole. But this activity is more than just a fact-finding exercise for the teacher. By co-operating in this way they become aware of *each other's* ideas and expectations and see their own requirements within the context of the whole group, thereby establishing to what extent they are shared by the others (does 'We want more grammar' really mean 'I want more grammar'?). More importantly, a group identity and sense of co-operation, independent of the teacher, is established from the start.

4 Something to go home with

But let us not get carried away. These people of varying backgrounds, personalities and perspectives we know in advance have at least one thing in common: they have come to improve their French and, therefore, by the end of the class, will be rather unhappy if they haven't learnt something in French they didn't know already. What you teach them will to some extent be based on how they fared during the ice-breaker. If you did a name chain the chances are at this level that their use of verb tenses may be a little suspect and need some straightening out. If your ice-breaker session took place over a glass of wine they may need to be taught some opening gambits and social chit-chat, such as 'Ça vous ennuie si je fume?', 'Vous venez souvent ici?' or 'Tenez, voilà Jacques qui vient d'arriver!'

Unit by unit

Each unit in this Guide for Teachers corresponds to a chapter in the user's book and the relevant radio programme.

The suggestions made in this book reflect my own teaching experience and beliefs and are not intended to be swallowed whole! Most are geared towards *communication* and *interaction*.

Each unit contains:
1 a list of new structures and exponents;
2 a list of structures and exponents where revision may be necessary, with reference either to earlier units or to **A Vous La France!**;
3 Tips for exploiting the materials;
4 Ideas – further ways of practising language covered in the chapter through games, songs or simulations. (Each simulation will take at least two $1\frac{1}{2}$ hour sessions.)
5 Where appropriate, in indication of a good moment for a Say what you want session. (A Say what you want session will take up a $1\frac{1}{2}$ hour class.)
6 For next time – activities or tasks for students to do before starting the next chapter. Important – allow time at the beginning of the next session to discuss these tasks. A student is likely to feel that his/her time had been wasted if you do not do so.

Book List

Theory   BAER, E. R. ed. *Teaching languages* BBC Publications, 1976
CURRAN, C. A. *Community language learning*
KRASHEN, S. D. *Second language acquisition and second language learning* Pergamon Press, 1981.
SIDWELL, D. ed. *Teaching languages to adults* CILT Publications 1984.
Practice   HADFIELD, J. *Harrap's communication games* Harrap, 1984.
JONES, B. ed. *Using authentic resources in teaching French* CILT Publications, 1984.
JONES, L. *Eight simulations: for upper-intermediate and more advanced students of English* Participator's and Controller's books. Cambridge University Press, paperback 1983.

1 Voici Biarritz

Structures and exponents:

aimer	bien
	beaucoup
	assez

ne pas aimer	tellement
	trop
	du tout

plaire	à quelqu'un
ne pas déplaire	

adorer
détester
avoir horreur de

trouver ça	très (très) bien
	affreux

ne pas pouvoir supporter

plus . . .	que
moins . . .	
aussi . . .	
pas si . . .	

On (ne) peut (pas) faire

To be revised: The present tense Chapter 7 p153 Ex 4
A Vous La France! Chapter 10 p207 Ex 10

Tips

1   Bring in a large (Michelin) map of France and point out Biarritz, Bayonne, L'Auvergne and other places 'visited' during the course.

2   'Jigsaw' listening with dialogues 1, 2 and 4 (jigsaw reading if equipment unavailable). Divide the class into three groups. As a

modification to **Avez-vous bien compris?** the first group is told they will be working on the interview with *la personne qui est en vacances*, the second with *la personne qui habite Paris 8 mois de l'année* and the third group will work with *la personne qui est grand-mère*. Play all three dialogues to the whole class. Each group has to identify its dialogue and then answer the question: 'Qu'est-ce que la personne aime surtout à Biarritz?' Re-mix groups for information exchange.

3 Brainstorm the class on ways of expressing 'likes' gleaned from the listening exercise. Write them on the board as they come up.

4 Ask students to write a list of things they like about this town individually. Re-form the same groups as for (2) above to discuss their lists.

5 If your town has a French twin, compare it with Biarritz. If not, compare Biarritz with your town. Do this as a class discussion.
Write up
plus ...	
moins ...	
aussi ...	
pas si ...	*que*
meilleur	
mieux	
pire	

as they come up.

6 Refer back to the map and give them a general knowledge 'lecturette' using superlatives: *la* ville *la* plus peuplée, c'est . . . la meilleure cuisine, c'est . . ., etc.
Then go through **Pour en savoir plus** 2 with them.

7 *Group Work:* Discuss the equivalent places in Britain to those mentioned in the lecturette (eg *quelle est la ville la plus peuplée de la Grande Bretagne?* etc). In plenary compare the results of the groups.

8 *In pairs:* do **Activité** 1a.

9 *In fours: Quelle activité est la plus difficile, chere* etc taking the adjectives from **Activité** 2. Feed in *bien, plus, beaucoup, moins*. As a class come to a consensus on *l'activité la plus difficile, chère,* etc.

10 *Discussion:* 'Est-ce qu'*on peut* faire ces activités dans notre ville?' (Practice of *on peut/on ne peut pas*).

In pairs: **Activité** 4.

Ideas
1 Set up a general knowledge panel game: 'Records'. One student is adjudicator with the Guinness Book of Records (French version if possible). Two panels challenge each other with questions such as

'Quel est le fleuve le plus long du monde?'. Teams should know the answer to their questions, but bluffing is allowed. One point for a correct answer, another point when a bluff is called successfully.

2 Play some short pieces of French music, for example, Brel, Brassens, Berlioz, Piaf, Jean Michel Jarre, Chedid, etc. Pause after each piece for the student's opinions:

J'adore
J'ai horreur de | *ça!*
J'aime bien

At the end decide as a group on 'le meilleur morceau'.

1 For next time
Do **A l'écoute**

2 Bring any information you can find on this town.

2 L'Auvergne

Saying where a place is situated
Talking about distances and directions
Describing where you live

Structures and exponents:

être situé			. . . km de
être	à		. . . mètres d'altitude
se situer			

Numbers from 100 to 999,000

Years: en | mil neuf | cent quarante quatre
        | dix-neuf |

(dix-neuf cent . . . used only for past years)

faire + measurement
for example: l'eau fait 30°

	sud	
au	sud-est	de
	nord	
	nord-ouest, etc	

| dans le | Sud |
| | Nord-Est, etc |

To be revised: Numbers to 100

Idea: Bingo – teacher calls out numbers in first game. Winner of
each game calls out subsequently. The competitors should call
'J'ai fini!' instead of 'Bingo!'. It might be less individually
competitive to play in pairs, 'On a fini!' being the catchphrase.
To save time you could use only even or only odd numbers.

Tips

1 Go through some numbers above 100 to check they know how to
form them. Refer to **Pour en savoir plus** 1b. Play Bingo as above
but add two zeros to all the numbers, for example 1700, 5800.

2 As an introduction to expressing measurements and statistics give a short lecture (two minutes) on this town or its French twin, giving, for example:

its distance from London/Glasgow/Belfast/Paris;
its population;
its average temperature;
the dimensions of a famous landmark;
and so on.

Recapitulate some of the figures. Get the students to repeat them chorally.

3 *Listening:* dialogue 2 with the 'adjoint au maire' de Chaudes-Aigues. Set the scene and ask the following pre-questions in French:

'Chaudes-Aigues se situe à combien de kilomètres de St Flour?' (Write up the two names)
'Chaudes-Aigues est située à quelle altitude?'
'L'eau chaude, à quoi sert-elle?'
'Combien de personnes viennent faire une cure chaque année?'

Play the cassette twice. Students compare their answers with the person nearest to them. Check answers. Play the cassette again, pausing after each figure for repetition.

4 Go through **Pour en savoir plus** 1, 2 and 3. Point out the differences in French in using the *virgule* for decimals and the gap for thousands.

5 *Reading:* Le Viaduc de Garabit. In groups of three (using a dictionary where necessary) each group has to decide, in English if they wish, what is the most impressive figure – *le chiffre le plus impressionnant* – then bring the class together and discuss, in French, each group's decision.

6 Spend plenty of time on the pronunciation section dealing with –*ille*.

Ideas

1 *Group activity.* Bring in objects or pictures of objects (for example, a brick, a bottle, etc), for one person to describe to the rest of the group of four or five. Each person has a turn and the group has to see whose object is identified by the others in the shortest time. Pre-teach vocabulary such as *rond, carré, en plastique/acier*, etc *ça sert à . . ., il/elle fait 15 cm de long . . .* and so on.

2 *Simulation:* Notre Ville. Two or three groups each prepare a radio programme for French consumption, to be recorded on to a cassette, on 'our town'. If you have video recording facilities they could make a television programme. If you are using video, I suggest you operate the camera so that you are seen as part of the project rather than sitting in judgement.

Each group should have a producer, one or two presenters, an interviewer, interviewees (as themselves) and scriptwriters. The groups themselves will decide who does what. The producer is the organiser and motivator of the project.

They will use materials collected themselves beforehand and these should cover geography and climate, famous buildings and facilities. The interviews will be along the lines of 'how long have you lived here?' and 'what do you think of the place?'.

The final programme should be no longer than 10 minutes. Stress the importance of keeping to French until the simulation is over. The groups may number anything from five to ten depending on the number of presenters and interviewers.

For the whole of the simulation *do not correct any errors*. You may want to note them for reference during the feedback. The timescale will be more or less as follows:

Setting up simulation and forming groups	15 minutes
Deciding on roles	5 minutes
Preparation of programme – writing of scripts, preparation of interviews, editing	60 minutes
Rehearsing lines	10 minutes
	1h 30

Recording (three programmes)	30 minutes
Feedback – English permitted – viewing, error analysis, discussion of tasks	60 minutes
	1h 30

Total: 3 hours (two sessions)

For next time
1   Activités

2   Writing – Write a paragraph describing le Viaduc de Garabit in sentence form from the data given in the chapter.

3 Un jour comme les autres

Saying what you do each day
Saying what you have to do
Talking about time

Structures and exponents:

Je dois | + *infinitive*
Il faut |

Il faut + *subjunctive*

The subjunctive mood

mettre du temps

Adverbs of frequency – souvent, toujours, etc

To be revised: Telling the time – Pour en savoir plus 2b
A vous la France! Chapter 6
Reflexive verbs in the present tense
A vous la France! Chapter 13 p260

Tips

1 Check the students' mastery of time-telling including the 24-hour clock.
2 *Listening:* Jigsaw listening with dialogues I (Christophe). 2 (Isabelle) and 5 (le boulanger) – up to '. . . Voilà la journée type du boulanger'. Set the scene by describing your journée type ('Je me lève à 7h, . . . je travaille jusqu'à . . .') etc, and perhaps inviting someone to describe theirs. Distribute photocopies of *figure 2* and divide the students into three groups.

	Heure de se lever	Activité du matin	Heure du déjeuner	Activité de l'après-midi	Activité du soir
Christophe					
Isabelle					
Le boulanger					

Figure 2

Group A will work on *la personne qui ne travaille pas l'après-midi (le boulanger)*, group B with *la personne qui aime jouer au tennis (Christophe)* and group C will work on *la personne qui a un parcours à faire tous les jours*. Play all three dialogues once for each to identify their character (play them in the order on *Figure 2*).

Give out the three cassettes (or copies of the three dialogues if you are exploiting them as a jigsaw reading). Tell them that there may not be answers for all the boxes but do not say which.

Re-mix the groups so that all the information may be exchanged (see *Figure 1*, page 12). This will generate lots of practice in question-forming in the third person singular.

Play all three dialogues again, pausing at the point relevant to everyone's answers.

3 *Discussion in groups:* 'Lequel des trois mène la vie la plus difficile?' A spokesman for the group then reports back on their discussion and conclusions to the others. This should provide good revision of the comparatives and superlatives.

4 *Pair work:* for practice in forming questions and answers in the first and second person singular ask them to form pairs and to write the name of their partner in the fourth box under *le boulanger* in *Figure 2*, and then get the relevant information from their partner.

5 Go through the **Pour en savoir plus** sections on *devoir, il faut* and the subjunctive. Do the relevant **Essayez donc!** exercises.

6 In groups of three, a similar exercise to 3 above, except that the *trois en question* should be the three people they each interviewed in 4 above. Encourage them to use 'il/elle doit faire . . .' and 'il faut qu'il/elle fasse . . .'. The reporting back session will be fun!

7 *Pronunciation:* as **A l'écoute** introduces many new words, go through their pronunciation. Have the group repeat them chorally.

Ideas

1 What's my line? – get pairs to prepare a *journée type* for someone with a particular job, consulting the teacher where necessary for certain expressions or vocabulary. They then read it out – for the others to guess – using the first person singular.

2 This is a good point to have the first 'Say what you want' session. It is *very* important to explain fully with mechanics and the reasoning behind it (see page 8). There may well be long silences in the recording phase. Don't be tempted into filling them! The group is in control.

For next time

1 The **A l'écoute** section.
2 'Write a paragraph on "la journée type" of the person you interviewed.'
3 'Try to remember as many names of professions and trades as you can in French.'
4 Ask the students to bring some of their holiday snaps – ones with people in them.

4 Biographies

Telling people about your life and job

Structures and exponents:

Present tense with depuis
Perfect tense with pendant

The PERFECT TENSE including être verbs and reflexives
The IMPERFECT TENSE

| être | mécanicien |
| | fonctionnaire, etc |

To be revised: if more work on the perfect tense is needed, refer to A vous la France! Chapters 12 (avoir verbs) and 13 (être verbs). Chapter 14 covers the imperfect tense.

Tips

1   Have a 'brainstorming' session with the class for the names of jobs in French. Write them up.

2   *Listening:* the five snippets of people giving their jobs. Before playing them ask: 'Que font ces cinq personnes dans la vie?'. Play the tape twice, then a third time, pausing after the name of the job. Add each one to the list on the board as they come up. You will probably have to explain *aide-soignante*, *cadre* and *surveillante* (and also *le standard*).

3   Go through the list of jobs in **Pour en savoir plus** 1. Also make sure the students know their jobs in French.

4   Go through the explanation of the perfect and imperfect tenses – **Pour en savoir plus** 3. You may want to supplement the **Essayez donc!** exercises with some from **A vous la France!** 12, 13 and 14.

5   *Listening:* the seventh snippet, Serge. Ask 'Pourquoi est-ce que Serge est devenu agriculteur?'. Play it a second time, pausing after

each verb for choral repetition. Write them up as follows:

J'ai fait	Je suis né	Je me suis installé
J'ai arrêté	Je suis parti	
J'ai trouvé	J'y suis resté	
	Je suis revenu	

L'enseignement ne me plaisait pas.
Des conditions qui m'étaient favorables.

Discuss why the different tenses are used here.

6 Go through **Pour en savoir plus** 3b – *il y a/ça fait/depuis* and **Essayez donc!**.

7 *Listening*: Marie-Christine and the *mineur*. For the interview with Marie-Christine ask the pre-question: 'Depuis combien de temps est-ce qu'elle vit à Bayonne?' (*Toute sa vie*). Play the cassette twice. The second time stop after '. . . depuis que je suis née,' and explain the use of *depuis que* + perfect tense.

For the interview with the miner ask 'Depuis combien de temps est-ce qu'il ne travaille plus?' (*7 ans*) and then 'Il a quel âge?' (*64 ans*). Be careful! The students may well disagree with you if they have *depuis* + present tense and *pendant* + perfect tense mixed up. Clarify it if necessary.

8 **Activité** 2: Instead of writing information about themselves in the space provided they should interview each other and write down the answers for other people. Everyone should interview at least two other people. Photocopy and use *Figure 3*.

Nom			
Prénom			
Age			
Né(e) à			
Domicilé(e) à			
Domicile précédent			
Profession			
Depuis quand?			
Célibataire			
Marié(e)/divorcé(e)			
Veuf/veuve			
Depuis quand?			
Enfants			

Figure 3

Before starting this activity, go through every category and check that they know how to ask the relevant question.

When everyone has interviewed at least two other people, bring them back together and invite volunteers to read out some of the information gathered.

Ideas

1 Having asked your students to bring their holiday photos, get them to show them to each other in groups of three. This will give them lots of practice in the use of the imperfect tense for giving background information, for example 'On était à 30 kilomètres de Barcelone', or 'Là, je mangeais du cous-cous', as well as the perfect tense in talking about what *happened* after the photo was taken, for example, 'On est parti le lendemain'. Make sure that they are aware of the difference before they begin – feed them with questions such as 'Qu'est-ce que tu faisais à Rome?', 'Tu étais où, là?' or 'Où est-ce que tu es allé(e) après?'. As always, 'a picture is worth a thousand words', so let it run!

2 As an alternative to tip no 8 above, if you have a more confident and sociable class, you may feel that the form is too rigid and prefer simply to leave them to find out as much as they can about at least two other people. You may want to have them standing up and 'mingling'.

3 For more practice of the imperfect and also names of jobs, a variation on 'What's my line?' – 'What used to be my line'!

Write on cards 10 or 20 different jobs. Form the class into two 'panels' with one person answering with only 'Oui' or 'Non' questions about the job he used to do, either real or taken from one of the cards chosen at random.

Each person in the panel takes turns in asking one Yes/No question. If the person whose past job they are trying to guess answers no, the other panel takes over. One can only guess when it is one's turn to ask a question, and, of course, an incorrect guess hands the initiative over to the other side.

For next time

1 'Write a short paragraph on one of the people you interviewed. Use only the information gathered at the time.'

2 Ask them to bring the following:

un petit bol	du sel
une petite cuillère	un citron
deux oeufs	un peu d'huile

Discuss what they think these might be needed for.

(Alternatively – if cooking is not your strong point – set them some other practical tasks, for example, wiring a plug. Make sure they bring in whatever is necessary.)

5 A votre service

Asking for help
Giving directions
Giving instructions

Structures and exponents:

Où se trouve *la* cabine téléphonique *la* plus proche?
    le supermarché   *le* plus proche?

Vous pourriez m'indiquer . . . ?

Giving instructions using:

1 Vous/tu + present tense
2 The infinitive (written)

Qu'est-ce qu'il faut que je fasse?

Une fois que vous avez (fait), vous (faites)

Direct and indirect object pronouns

Use of *si*

To be revised: Use of il faut + infinitive for instructions
A vous la France! Chapter 9.
Giving directions – à droite/gauche
              sur votre droite/gauche
                  la droite/gauche
              tout droit
              la première   à gauche
                  deuxième, etc droite
A vous la France! Chapter 9.

Tips

1 Check the students' ability both to give *and* to understand the directions outlined above under 'To be revised'. Revise the adjectives of position:

à côté	de
en face	
près	
devant	
derrière	See **Ideas**.

2 *Listening:* dialogues 1, 2 and 3 with Ermi. In pairs: 'Mettez une croix pour indiquer où se déroule chacune de ces trois conversations.' Photocopy *Figure 4.*

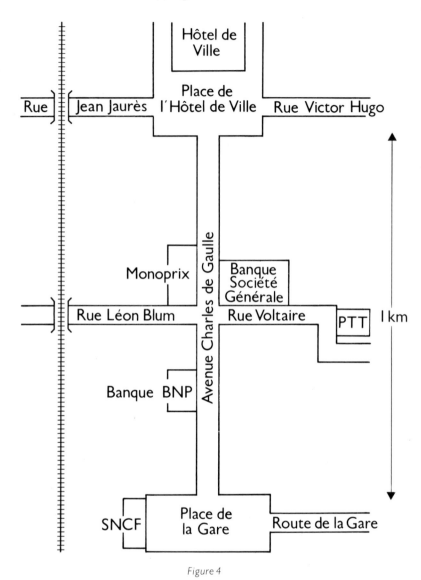

Figure 4

Answers:
1 Dans la route de la Gare
2 Sur le coin de la Rue Voltaire et l'Avenue Charles de Gaulle
3 Au bureau des PTT

Play dialogues 1 and 2 twice and dialogue 3 only once, up to '. . . c'est le tarif urgent'. It is important that, after completing the task, answers are given and compared *orally* so that positional words and phrases (*à côté de*, *tout de suite après*, *au bout de la rue*, etc) are practised.

Isolate the question 'Où se trouve la cabine téléphonique la plus proche?' on the tape. Explain that this is a more 'elegant' form of the perfectly acceptable 'Est-ce qu'il y a une cabine téléphonique près d'ici?', although the former *may* provoke a friendlier reply. Put forward a few other places, for example *l'hôtel*, *la pharmacie*, *le tabac*, with which they might use the same question and let them get used to changing 'le plus proche' to 'la plus proche' accordingly. Give them plenty of choral repetition.

3 *Jigsaw Reading:* The telephone leaflet in **Activité** 1. As with a jigsaw listening, break the class into three groups (see *Figure 1*, page 12).

Group 1 will work on the left-hand half of the leaflet under 'Comment téléphoner vers l'Etranger depuis la France?' Give them the following questions on a separate piece of paper.

> 1 What do you have to do to make a telephone call abroad from France?
>
> 2 When are the off-peak rates in operation for phoning to England? What about weekends?

Group 2 will work on the top right-hand section – the list of 'Pays' and 'Indicatifs'. Their questions are as follows:

> 1 Are there any countries for which one doesn't start by dialling 19?
>
> 2 Which countries benefit from an off-peak rate?
>
> 3 What is the French for: the United Kingdom, East Germany, Cyprus, Lebanon, Trinidad?

Group 3 will work on the bottom right-hand section under 'Quelques Conseils Pratiques'.

> 1 What does one do about the first zero in STD codes, for example 051 (Liverpool) and 0483 (Guildford)?
>
> 2 What is French for: 'to dial a number'?
>   'time difference'?
>
> 3 If you don't get a ringing tone after dialling the number, why shouldn't you immediately dial the number again?

When the tasks are completed, re-mix the groups and distribute the following task paper to all the groups (still in English).

29

> 1 Exchange your information *without* showing the others in your group the section you studied.
>
> 2 How would you phone Nottingham (0602) 393173 from France? At what times would you avoid phoning?

Finally play the second part of dialogue 3 again to give them the pleasure of understanding the instructions given. Before doing so, pre-set the following question (in English):

What is the difference between 'les cabines téléphoniques' one might find in the street and those found in a post office? (In a post office one pays the clerk afterwards.)

4 *Pronunciation:* Go through the following vocabulary of the telephone for pronunciation practice. This is particularly important as the students have met them only in written form (apart from those mentioned in dialogue 3) and many of the terms are similar in spelling to English words, but with a very different pronunciation:

la tonalité	composer
l'indicatif	un abonné
la communication (*the call*)	décrocher
un décalage horaire	le tarif réduit
mettre une pièce	raccrocher

5 *Listening:* dialogue 4, Ermi and the call box. Exploit this dialogue more extensively by giving out (or writing up) the list of instructions below and asking one pre-question: 'Est-ce que le téléphone marche ou non?'.

> **Mode d'emploi**
>
> 1 Décrocher
> 2 Mettre une pièce
> 3 Attendre la tonalité
> 4 Composer le numéro
> 5 Pour remboursement, appuyer sur le bouton noir.

Figure 5

6 Play the dialogue through without stopping.

Practice of 'Qu'est-ce qu'il faut que je fasse?' and 'Une fois que . . .'.

In pairs, one person has a copy of the above 'Mode d'emploi', the others asks questions as in the model below:

A: Qu'est-ce qu'il faut que je fasse d'abord?
B: D'abord, tu décroches.
A: Une fois que j'ai décroché, qu'est-ce qu'il faut que je fasse?
B: Une fois que tu as décroché, tu mets la pièce.
A: Une fois que j'ai mis la pièce, qu'est-ce qu'il faut que je fasse?
etc.

For further practice see **Pour en savoir plus** Ig **Essayez donc!** (using *vous*).

7 Go through all of **Pour en savoir plus** with the students. Have them do the **Essayez donc!** exercises in pairs.

8 *Pronunciation:* The Pronunciation section of this chapter deals with the important *u/ou* distinction. This is one of the most difficult pair of phonemes for English people to get right, and because both sounds are so common, they are a common source of confusion (for example, *dessus/dessous*; *tu vas bien/tout va bien*). Work here will pay dividends for them in the future. Let them see the position of your lips and tongue. You might even prepare copies of a cassette of you reading a series of 'minimal pairs' (*tu . . . tout*; *vu . . . vous*; *dessus . . . dessous*, etc). Leave gaps for them to repeat. Ideally they could then take them home and record themselves for comparison.

Pair work: All the **Activités**. Having them do **Activité** 4 as mini-dialogues, taking turns at asking similar questions using the different forms:

Pourriez-vous m'indiquer
Où se trouve | la banque la plus proche, etc

Ideas

1 For practice at understanding directions photocopy *figure 6* and dictate directions in answer to questions put by the students. For example, in answer to a request for directions to 'la banque la plus proche', you may direct them on the map to building number 4. (Number 10 may be 'la pharmacie la plus proche'.) Students work individually to your directions and then compare results afterwards in pairs using positional phrases, for example 'la banque est en face de la pharmacie', etc.
There is also an opportunity here to practise direct objects and to introduce past participle agreement with 'j'ai mis', which changes pronunciation when an 'e' is added. When going through the answers to the question
'Où est-ce que vous avez mis la banque?'
le musée?'
etc
individuals will then reply:

'Je l'ai mise au numéro 4.'
'Je l'ai mis au numéro 6.', etc

Explain the rule at the beginning and point out that pronunciation of most past participles is unaffected.

2 On your next visit to France bring back anything with instructions on it – soup packets, medicine bottles, 'modes d'emploi' for consumer goods – and have students in small groups of three or four try and work them out.

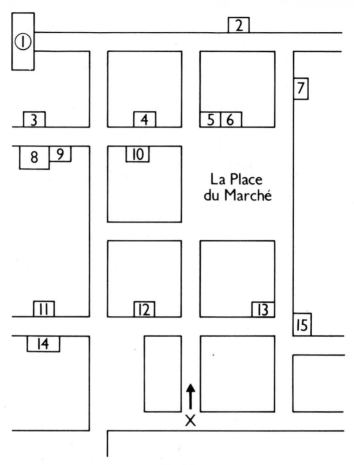

Figure 6

3 *Telephone Language:* Write up some model phrases for use when telephoning perhaps in the form of a 'model' dialogue:

Allo, oui

> Bonjour, est-ce que je peux parler à Michel ?

C'est lui

> C'est de la part de qui?
> ... Ne quittez pas.

> Michel n'est pas là en ce moment. Je peux lui laisser un message ?

Oui, vous pouvez lui dire que ... ?

> Non, merci. Je rappellerai ce soir/ tout à l'heure.

If you have telephone extensions in your centre you may be able to arrange to use the internal system to practise talking over the phone.

If not, ask them to phone one another at home before next time (in French, of course!).

4 *A Practical Session:* Teach them how to make 'la mayonnaise', wire a plug, etc.

The great value of this exercise is that by seeing the instructions enacted by you and by doing the same, the task in hand becomes more important than the form of the language used. These are vital conditions for language acquisition.

5 This is a good point for a 'Say what you want' session.

For next time

1 Ask them to telephone each other in French (see Idea 3 above).

2 Ask them to go to a superstore which has labels and instructions in both English and French and find out the French for the following:

To avoid suffocation, keep this wrapper away from children.

For refund, do not remove.

Hip
Waist   Size . . .   Average
Collar

Do not iron.
Remove before use.
Open and reseal here.
100% cotton. Reshape while damp.

3 Do the **A l'écoute** section.

4 Bring an item of clothing for next session.

6 Quand le choix est difficile

Explaining your needs
Making choices

Structures and exponents:

J'aimerais
Je voudrais $+$ noun $+$ qui $+$ subjunctive
Il me faudrait

Pourriez-vous me montrer ce que vous avez en . . . ?

Lequel, etc
Celui-ci/là, etc

To be revised: A vous la France! Chapter 8 covers the following:
Celui-ci, etc and lequel, etc.
Quantifiers: assez, trop, très, etc.
Comparatives: plus, moins (see also France Extra!
Chapter 7).
Specifying size, colour and material.

Tips

1 There is an enormous amount of vocabulary involved in describing clothes. Having the students bring in garments of their own is a more interesting way of presenting it than most and certainly fun.

   Ask those who have brought something to hand it to you. Describe each one beginning 'C'est à qui?' and write up the key phrases, vocabulary and particularly intermediary colours such as 'asperge' or 'vert-bouteille' as well as adjectives describing patterns like à carreaux; rayé; bariolé etc. Include some garments of your own that will make sure you cover the vocabulary.

   As they will have little hope of retaining such a large amount of vocabulary give them time to write it all down. Then with each garment hidden from view describe them again, one by one, for each individual to claim with the phrase 'C'est à moi, celui-là/celle-là!' Do not name the garment, they must recognise it only from your description.

2 Listening: The last part of dialogue 3 (Nicole) from '. . . alors, pourriez-vous me montrer ce que vous avez en rouge et en blanc?'

1 Comment est la robe que Nicole n'a pas achetée? Pourquoi est-ce qu'elle a choisi l'autre?

2 Quel est le prix de la robe? Qu'est-ce qu'elle en pense?

Play the tape once, then check the answers.
Play the segment a second time, pausing after the following useful phrases for repetition:
'. . . pourriez-vous me montrer ce que vous avez en rouge et en blanc?'
'Celle-ci certainement ira très bien.'

(Introduce **Ça** | **vous va bien** _– It suits you._)
                   | te

'. . . _soit_ pour une personne un peu plus forte, _soit_ une personne un peu plus mince.'
(showing them how simple 'soit . . . soit' is to use)

'C'est le prix que je voulais mettre.'
(How would they say 'it's a bit too expensive'?)

'Vous pouvez me faire un paquet-cadeau, s'il vous plaît?'

3 _Shoes:_ Footwear, too, has its own vocabulary. It even has its own word for 'size' – _pointure._ Using real examples, taken from your own shoe collection(!), introduce the following words and phrases:

(demi-) pointure	la semelle
talon	les espadrilles
à haut talon	les sandales
à talon plat	les bottes =
compensé	les barrettes
le cuir	richelieu (_lace up_)
le cirage	les lacets

In pairs, have them describe each other's shoes. Re-mix the pairs several times so that they have plenty of practice.

4 _Listening:_ dialogue 1, extensive listening. Set only one pre-question: 'Décrivez les espadrilles qu'a choisies Ermi'. Play the complete dialogue twice without stopping.

5 Go through all of **Pour en savoir plus** including the **Essayez donc!** exercises to be done in pairs.
    When practising _celui-ci_, etc, point out that _celui/celle(s)/ ceux-là_ are more commonly used than _celui-ci_, the latter (_celui-ci_) having only a contrastive use with _celui-là_ when distinguishing two objects, one of which is nearer than the other. Also point out that _celui-là_ is almost always condensed to _s'ui-là_ in speech, while _celui-ci_ is never shortened.
    The point made in 1d – that the subjunctive is used after _que_ or _qui_ when dealing with a thing or idea which exists (for the moment) only in one's mind – is fundamental to understanding its use. However, as with most grammatical 'nuances', they will not grasp this idea if you do not give them _lots of examples._

Ideas

1 For the practice of *celui-là*, etc, the subjunctive and much of the vocabulary presented in this unit, 'sell off' all the clothes that have been brought in. The students will initiate using phrases such as:

Je voudrais J'aimerais Il me faudrait	une	chemise robe	qui que	soit aille avec je puisse mettre avec

2 Magazines such as 'Marie-Claire', 'Cosmopolitain' and 'Elle' are ideal sources of (jigsaw) reading material, *well illustrated* with glossy pictures, covering all types of clothes – just look under 'La Mode'.

3 *Simulation:* 'Le Salon du Prêt-a-Porter'. The students will be either boutique owners or *représentant(e)s*. Each *représentant(e)* will be trying to persuade the boutique owners to stock their goods in the next financial year. They will be armed with one of the fashion magazines which will represent their collection and each will have a different magazine and therefore a different *collection*. Each boutique is run by two people who have to discuss with the sales rep in turn the merits of various garments and decide which to take, and how many. Give them a budget of, say, 100000 Francs.

There should be the same number of reps as boutiques, ie twice as many owners as reps, so that as the reps examine each 'stand', armed with either 'Elle', 'Cosmo', 'Marie-Claire' or 'Femme', everyone will be engaged in negotiation at the same time, at least at the beginning.

It will be interesting to compare each boutique's 'collection' at the end.

For next time

1 'Listen to all three dialogues on shopping, read the vocabulary lists and do the **Avez-vous bien compris?** exercises.'

2 'Do the **A l'écoute** section.'

3 'Bring a photo of you as a child!'

7 Que de changements dans la vie...

Contrasting past and present

Structures and exponents:

The imperfect tense

ne . . . jamais
ne . . . plus
ne . . . personne   personne ne . . .
ne . . . rien   rien ne . . .

ne . . . plus │ personne
              │ jamais
              │ rien

Use of y
Use of toujours
Use of souvent
Use of même
Use of alors │ que (maintenant)
       tandis │

To be revised: The formation of the imperfect tense –
France Extra! Chapter 4
A vous la France! Chapter 14
Forming negatives – *A vous la France!* p.317

Tips

1 Assuming most of the students have brought an old photo of
   themselves, give out the form, *Figure 7*, below.

Nom de la personne		
Description de la photo		
Age à l'époque		
Domicile		
Situation familiale		
Signalement		
Etat d'esprit		
La vie à l'époque		
Passe-temps		

Figure 7

Before beginning check that they are familiar with the imperfect tense and revise if necessary.

Using a photo of yourself, preferably as a child, but at 10 years old at least, go through the questions one might ask in order to fill in the form for someone else and answer the questions for yourself.

Description de la photo:	'Qui a pris la photo?' 'Tu étais/vous étiez où?' 'Qu'est-ce que tu faisais?' 'Qui sont les autres personnes dans la photo?' etc 'Qu'est-ce que tu portais?'
Age à l'époque:	'Tu avais quel âge?'
Domicile:	'Tu habitais où?'
Situation familiale:	'Tu avais des frères/des soeurs?'
Signalement:	'Comment étais-tu?' (*maigre, grand(e)* *pour mon âge, etc*) 'Tu faisais combien?'
Etat d'ésprit:	'Tu étais heureux/heureuse?'
La vie à l'époque:	'Comment c'était, la vie à l'époque?'
Passe-temps:	'Qu'est-ce que tu aimais faire?' ('Qu'est-ce que tu n'aimais pas?')

In pairs, ask them to fill in the form for their partner (in note form). You may feel it necessary to draw *Figure* 7 on the board and fill it in for yourself while going through the questions.

Finally invite *volunteers* to present a profile of their partner. Make it a question and answer session so that the above questions (and others) may be practised in the third person singular.

2   Go straight to **Pour en savoir plus** I for further explanation.

3   Discussion of their town 20 years ago, as an introduction to contrasting past and present.

Introduce the phrase   *alors* ⎱ *que*
                                    tandis ⎰

maintenant . . . and *autrefois*.

4   *Listening Comprehension* – Dialogue I
Explain who Henri is and set the following pre-question
'Comment est-ce que la clientèle de l'Hôtel du Palais d'il y a 20 ans est différente de celle d'aujourd'hui?'

Play the dialogue once and then, before playing it a second time, ask them to write two headings 'Autrefois' and 'Maintenant' in order that they write down answers to the pre-question in two lists. After the second playing tabulate the answers on the board in the same way. Write them up *in the words of the students* who give them to you, for example:

Autrefois	*Maintenant*
Il y avait beaucoup d'anglais	Ce sont des hommes d'affaires qui viennent.
Les clients restaient longtemps	Ce sont des courts séjours

Add to the list phrases that came out of the discussion 3 above on their town. In pairs ask them to make sentences of the form *'Autrefois . . . alors que maintenant . . .'*. This would be a good moment to introduce *ne . . . plus* if they haven't met it already. Practise chorally the sentence, *Il n'y en a plus*, particularly with attention to the correct stress. Try and get them to link it all together smoothly. *Il n'y en a plus.*

5 (Optional) **Avez-vous bien compris?** exercise after Dialogue I.

6 In pairs **Activité** I. Introduce *il/elle n'y est plus* and *il/elle a disparu*.

7 The negatives. Go through **Pour en savoir plus** 2. Point out the position of *personne* in phrases in the perfect tense such as:
    je n'ai vu *personne*.
(cf je n'ai *rien* vu.
    je n'ai *pas* vu . . .
    je n'ai *jamais* vu . . .)

Ask them in pairs (not the same pairs as in 6 above) to translate the following:

I No one goes to the cinema any more.
2 I never used to do it.
3 I'll never do it again.
4 I didn't see anything at the fête.
5 I didn't see anyone at the fête.
6 Don't say anything to anyone.
7 Don't say anything else to anyone.
8 Nothing interests me.
9 There's no one left and there's nothing left.
10 I never used to meet anyone at work.

8 Use of *y*. Go through **Pour en savoir plus** 3 and **Essayez donc!** **Activité** 3.

9 *Le Mouvement Nationaliste Basque*. Do some background reading and give a short, simplified lecturette on its history. This will give them the necessary information and vocabulary to listen to Dialogues 2 and 3 at home. Ask them to find out how the separatist movement has affected Bayonne (in English).

Ideas
1 A *Say what you want session* in which they may, in view of what has gone before, be feeling nostalgic!

For next time
1 All the **Activités**.

2 'Write a profile of your partner at the time at which the photograph you have seen of him/her was taken. Use the notes you made in the form.'

8 La parole est aux jeunes

Talking about hopes, expectations and intentions
Making a date
Accepting and declining an invitation

Structures and exponents:

aller
espérer
compter   faire
avoir l'intention de

The future tense

The conditional tense

To be revised: Present tense of aller, avoir

Infinitives

Tips

1   Using an explanatory text of 'L'Education Nationale' up to
university level (for example, in *Allez France* BBC Publications
p. 122, or one written by yourself), introduce them to the French
education system.
   Begin by asking them about their own school memories – this is
also a way of revising areas covered in the last unit and the
vocabulary of jobs (*Qu'est-ce que vous vouliez devenir?*)

Exploit your text by breaking it into three parts covering:

1   de 2 ans à 11 ans
2   de 11 ans à 16 ans
le premier cycle (de la 6e à la 3e classe)
3   après 16 ans
le deuxième cycle et le baccalauréat

As a jigsaw reading *(see Figure 1)* give the three parts of the text
and the following questions:
1   When does compulsory education begin?
2   What kind of schools do younger children go to?
3   How long is *l'enseignement primaire*?
4   A child who is *en quatrième* in France would probably be in what

year in a British secondary school?

5　What is the minimum school leaving age?

6　What is the *BEPC*?

7　Why is the *baccalauréat* so important?

8　To what kind of school does one go to take it and in which year?

9　If you wanted to study Biology at university which *bac* would you take?

10　What is a more practical alternative to the *baccalauréat* for those not wanting to go to university?

In the jigsaw reading Group 1 would answer questions *1* to *3*, Group 2 would answer 4 to 6 and Group 3 questions 7 to 10. The remixed groups would then exchange information to complete the questionnaire.

　　You may feel that the whole exercise can be done in French, in which case the questionnaire should also be in French.

2　*Listening* – Introduce any vocabulary relating to education (for example *préparer; aller en fac*, etc) not already covered which they will need to understand dialogues 1 and 2 (Cécile and Virginie).

1　Introduce Virginie (dialogue 2) and set the pre-question: *'Qu'est-ce qu'elle veut faire plus tard?'*. Play the whole dialogue once (Answer: *'Elle veut devenir avocat'*). Then ask *'Qu'est-ce qu'il faut faire/étudier pour devenir avocat?'* (*'Il faut faire du droit'*).

2　Play the dialogue again and use the pause button to stop after each example of her future plans. Have them repeat chorally, then write it up.

3　Introduce Cécile with the question:

I　'Qu'est-ce qu'elle va étudier et où, lorsqu'elle aura son bac?'

II　'Est-ce qu'elle travaille sérieusement en ce moment?'

4　Proceed as in 2 above, adding examples of future intent to the list (including those in the present tense).

　　Highlight sentences with *si* . . . and *quand* . . . and explain that, unlike with 'when' in English, *quand* takes the future tense (for example, *quand tu l'auras, qu'est-ce que tu feras?*).

　　Point out that the present tense is often used (as in *je vais en fac à Paris*) to express *definite* plans already arranged for a given time: *je pars à huit heures; je travaille demain*.

3　Go through **Pour en savoir plus** 1 and 2. You may find it useful to point out that the difference between *Je pars pour Rome le 17* and *Je partirai pour Rome le 17* is roughly equivalent to the difference between 'I leave for Rome on the 17th' and 'I'll leave for Rome on the 17th', ie the first example is a fixed arrangement, while the second is more of a personal intention. Have them in pairs then consider **Pour en savoir plus** 2b **Essayez donc!** in that light.

4　*Listening* – Set up Dialogue 3 as follows: Cécile and Virginie meet by chance in the street. How pleased are they to see each other and what do they decide to do and when?'

　　Play the whole dialogue through once, and invite answers in English.

Before playing again the first half, ask them to think about how they expressed their pleasure at seeing each other. Play up to '*Ah, moi aussi*'.

Play the first half again and pause for choral repetition after *Ça fait longtemps que je t'ai pas vue*', '*Ben ouais, ça fait longtemps . . .*' and '*Ça me fait beaucoup plaisir de te voir là*'. Write them up.

Before playing the second half ask them to think about how they fix a date and set the pre-question: 'Why can't Cécile make next week?'.

As a conclusion to the listening exercise, write up Figure 8 on the board (without exponents taken from Dialogues 3 and 4) and ask them to read through Dialogues 3 and 4 giving you examples of the five functions.

5 Go through **Pour en savoir plus** 3 and 4, adding to the lists in *Figure 8*.

Chance meeting	Inviting	Declining (Giving a reason)	Accepting	Making an arrangement
Ça fait longtemps que je t'ai pas vu(e) Ça (me) fait plaisir de te (re)voir (là) Qu'est-ce que tu deviens?	On pourrait/ Ce serait possible de se voir . . .	Je pars en voyage J'ai des trucs à faire	Si tu veux Pourquoi pas? (less enthusiastic than English)	Où/ A quelle heure est-ce qu'on pourrait se donner rendez-vous? Je viendrai te chercher Je te passe un coup de téléphone/fil On se voit là-bas Il vaudrait mieux (qu'on aille . . .) C'est bon d'accord

Figure 8

Ideas

1 Prepare photocopies of the relevant week from a French *agenda*. Give them out and ask them to write in their actual commitments for next week (in French – help them if necessary). Then put them together in groups of 4. Say you can't do next week's class and ask them to arrange another day.

2 For practice of the conditional tense. This activity is in two parts. Prepare a list of names of everyone in the class. Make enough copies for everyone in the class, plus one for you to cut up. There should be a space of approximately I inch between each name. Then prepare a list of questions beginning '*Qu'est-ce que tu ferais si . . .*'. There should be the same number of questions as people in the class. Try and make them amusing or interesting. For example:

'*Qu'est-ce que tu ferais si, au moment de payer l'addition au restaurant, tu te rendais compte que tu avais laissé ta porte-monnaie/ton sac-à-main à la maison?*'

'Qu'est-ce que tu ferais si tu voyais un phantôme dans la nuit?'

'Qu'est-ce que tu ferais si un chat passait toute une nuit devant ta porte d'entrée?'

'Qu'est-ce que tu ferais si tu voyais quelqu'un voler un sac-à-main dans une foule?'

'Qu'est-ce que tu ferais si, ayant envoyé deux lettres, tu te rendais compte que tu t'étais trompé(e) d'envelopes?'

'Qu'est-ce que tu ferais si tu t'étais enfermé(e) dehors, ayant laissé une casserole sur le feu?'

'Qu'est-ce que tu ferais, si, au cours d'une conversation, tu te rendais compte que tu avais appelé la personne par un nom qui n'était pas le sien?' etc.

Phase I of the activity is to give everyone a list of names and one question. Each member of the class then asks that one question to everyone else and notes the answer against their name in the first person singular *'Je . . .'*.

For phase 2 give each person a slip of paper with the name of someone else in the group and a list of all the questions. Each person then asks other members of the group what the person on their slip of paper answered to their question in Phase I, thereby completing the questionnaire for the person on their slip without actually asking him. The exchange in Phase 2 would be:

'Quelle était votre question tout à l'heure?'

'C'était qu'est-ce que tu ferais si tu voyais un phantôme dans la nuit?'

'Alors, que ferait X s'il/si elle voyait un phantôme?'

'Il/elle hurlerait.'

See *Figure 9* if you are confused!

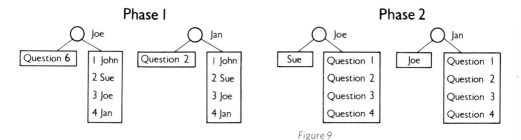

Figure 9

This activity generates an enormous amount of language activity. At the end collect in all the questionnaires, correct them and next time pin them up.

For next time

1 Answer all the *'Qu'est-ce que tu ferais si . . .'* questions for yourself – write the answers.

2 A l'écoute

9 A votre santé

Giving reasons for doing things
Explaining your motives
Talking about your health and how you feel

Structures and exponents:

parce que + verb clause
à cause de + noun
pour + infinitive

avoir se faire se casser se tordre se fouler	mal à	parts of the body

| avoir | un problème
un ennui | au niveau de | |

To be revised: More common parts of the body

avoir mal à . . .
A vous la France! Chapter 9, page 187
Medical directions
A vous la France! Chapter 9, Dialogues 5 and 6

Tips

1 *Jigsaw Reading – Le Système de Santé*. Break the text into three parts ending at ' . . . *la consultation et les médicaments*', '. . . *mais il paie beaucoup plus*' and '. . . *Grande Bretagne.*' Give a different section to each of groups 1, 2 and 3 and to everyone the following list of questions:

1 What is the French word for 'prescription'?
2 How much does a doctor's visit cost?
3 What is the purpose of *une feuille de maladie?* What does one do with it?
4 For a person in work, how much of his or her medical expenses does the State refund?
5 What is *une Mutuelle?*
6 How is *La Sécurité Sociale* funded?
7 What proportion of the French choose to 'go private'?
8 How can a British visitor to France get medical cover?

Group I will answer questions *I* to *4*, Group 2 will answer questions *5* and *6* and Group 3 will work on *7* and *8*. Remix the groups to exchange the information and answer all the questions.

Answer questions on vocabularly in the text. The following items will probably be new to them:

le congé de maladie
s'inscrire à ...
verser
remplir une fiche
se faire rembourser
salarié
cotiser
réclamer

Emphasise the point that under the French health system one always pays out first and that this is very expensive. Even the DHSS form only entitles one to reimbursement. You may feel it advisable to recommend private health insurance as the only way of eliminating any financial outlay at all.

2 *Jigsaw listening* – Explain what *une cure* is and have the students read the introductory paragraph to Dialogues I, 2 and 3.

Play all three dialogues to the three groups. Group I will work on 'the person who is mentally tired', Group 2 on 'the person who is there for three weeks' and Group 3 will listen to 'the person who also wants to lose weight'. The first listening exercise will be for each group to identify their extract. Then give the three groups their cassette and ask them to fill in their section of the table under **Avez-vous bien compris?**.

The groups then remix as in *Figure I* (page 12) to exchange information (in French) and complete the table.

3 Go through **Pour en savoir plus** 3. In pairs do **Essayez donc!**

4 **A l'écoute** – Get hold of *une feuille de maladie*, photocopy it and use it with the **A l'écoute** section from *'Alors, je vais tarifer l'ordonnance'*. Have the students follow *la pharmacienne*'s instructions. You could give them each an SS number.

5 Go through **Pour en savoir plus** I and 2. In pairs do **Activité** I.

Ideas

1 For further practice of 'Cause and Effect', tell the following story (from your hospital bed!). (See *figure 10* overleaf.) Encourage the students to take notes while you are narrating. (You may want to draw a pictorial representation as an aide-memoire – you don't need to be Rolf Harris!)

In pairs, using *Figure 10* as an aide-memoire, students ask each other:

'Pourquoi est-ce que ... s'est disputé(e) avec sa femme (son mari, son ami(e))

'Parce qu'il ne voulait pas lui prêter la voiture.'

'Pourquoi est-ce qu'il ('elle) a fait une promenade?'

'A cause de la dispute/Pour se calmer, etc.'

Students can also go on to make sentences in the past conditional tense, such as *'S'il n'avait pas oublié de mettre le réveil, il ne serait pas arrivé en retard pour son travail'*, or with *devoir*, such as *'Il aurait dû mettre le réveil'*, *'Il n'aurait pas dû se saouler'*, etc.

'Mon mari/ma femme/mon ami(e), l'autre soir, a voulu prendre ma voiture pour faire un tour et j'ai refusé. On s'est mis à se disputer à tel point que je suis sorti(e) faire une promenade jusqu'à une heure pour me calmer. En me couchant, j'ai oublié de mettre le réveil. Le lendemain le réveil n'a pas sonné et donc je suis arrivé(e) en retard pour mon travail. Mon patron m'a demandé pourquoi et, comme j'avais 'mal au cheveux' je l'ai traité d' 'imbécile' et bien sûr il m'a viré(e). Je suis allé(e) directement au café et je me suis saoulé(e) pour essayer d'oublier ce qui venait de m'arriver. Bêtement je suis rentré(e) à la maison avec la voiture. J'ai brûlé un feu rouge et quelqu'un m'est rentré dedans. Je me suis cassé(e) la jambe et me voilà en hôpital.'

Figure 10

For next time
Listen to Dialogues 4 and 5 and do the **Avez-vous bien compris?** exercise.

10 Du côté des femmes

Structures and exponents:

The language of agreeing and disagreeing, including:

j'estime	
je crois	que . . .
je suis convaincu	
je doute	

The pluperfect tense

venir de + infinitive

aucun/aucune
ne . . . aucun/aucune
ne . . . que

use of *en*

To be revised: The imperfect tense
France Extra! Chapters 4 and 7
A vous la France! Chapter 14

Tips

Note – Discussion is something which is difficult to 'stage'.
People very rarely have something strong to say just when you
want them to, particularly if you choose the subject. However,
introduce **Pour en savoir plus** I and explain that discussions,
particularly political ones are far more common in everyday life –
at work, at parties, etc – than in Britain. (That in itself may
provoke some discussion.) If discussions do develop during this
unit (more likely in small groups), let them run but do not try to
force them. Exchanges of views may occur spontaneously later in
the course, most probably in a *Say what you want* session.

1   Begin with **Pour en savoir plus** I and 2.

2 Listening – Mme Vermenouze. Set the scene and write up the following pre-questions:

1 What made Mme Vermenouze go out to work?
2 How old were her children and how old was she?
3 Why was it hard?
4 What did she end up doing?

Play the dialogue up to '. . . *c'est pas facile*'. Go through the above questions.
   Play the same segment of the dialogue again, pausing after each verb phrase for repetition and write them up on the board as below in three lists:

J'avais passé mon bac	Il fallait faire quelque chose	Je me suis renseignée
Je m'étais mariée jeune (Je venais de perdre mon mari), etc	Cela avait une utilité, etc	J'ai créé une petite agence, etc

On examining the three lists students should be able to see quite clearly the difference in use of the three tenses shown. The first list of verbs in the pluperfect + *je venais de . . .* will be new to them.
   Explain the mechanics of the formation of the pluperfect (the auxiliary verb of the perfect tense, *avoir* or *être*, is put into the imperfect form and the past participle is unchanged) and then refer them to **Pour en savoir plus** 3 and for the explanation of *venir de . . .* to **Pour en savoir plus** 4. Go through the **Essayez donc!** exercise as a class and clear up any confusion in general discussion. Deal with *venir de* separately. The best way to deal with it is to establish a direct semantic link between 'I have just done' and *je viens de faire* and between 'I had just done' and *je venais de faire*, pointing out that *je viens/venais de . . .* takes the infinitive, not the past participle.

3 Go back to the first part of Nicole's interview with Mme Vermerouze and isolate either from the cassette or from the written text the following phrases:

'la plus jeune des enfants n'avait que 10 ans, . . . un autre n'en avait que 15.'
'Aviez-vous une formation professionnelle à cette époque?' . . .
'Non, je n'en avais aucune.' '. . . donc de formation je n'en avais pas'.

Invite comment and questions on these structures and then go through **Pour en savoir plus** 5 and 6, having pairs do all the **Essayez donc!** exercises. (In the **Essayez donc!** exercise practising *en* and other object pronouns, give credit to anyone giving the answer '*J'ai envie d'y aller*' to number 1.)

4 Listening – More from Mme Vermenouze. Explain, in French, Mme Vermenouze's involvement with '*L'Association des Veuves* *dans Le Cantal'*, in preparation for a listening exercise with her answer to Nicole's last question *'Quels sont les problèmes en particulier qui affectent ces jeunes veuves?'*

Pre-teach the following vocabulary:

subitement	acquérir
une adhérente	se contenter de . . .
le monde salarial	
la formation	

Pre-question: 'Why do young widows so often end up doing lowly jobs?' Play the cassette from Nicole's last question (see above) to the end of the interview '. . . *s'organiser avec leurs enfants.*' Answer the pre-question and then break the class into groups of four to discuss the following question:

'Est-ce qu'un jeune veuf est forcément mieux équipé qu'une jeune veuve pour continuer une vie seul?'

Make sure there are both men and women in each group. Ask one member of each group to make notes of the discussion and its conclusion and also someone – not necessarily the same person – to be prepared to report back on the discussion to the rest of the class. Remind them, if necessary, of some of the expressions in **Pour en savoir plus** I.

Do not stop any discussions prematurely and do *not* correct during the activity. For the reporting session ask the spokesman only to present the conclusions of the group and invite comment from the others.

5 If the above procedure is successful another subject for discussion in small groups is one based on **Le saviez-vous?** – *'Les femmes en France'*:
'Est-ce que les femmes en France sont plus ou moins libérées que les femmes en Grande Bretagne?'

Ideas
Simulation – The Court Scene. An opportunity to practise all three past tenses.

Roles:
Le juge
Le Procureur
Le Défenseur
L'Accusé
Trois témoins à charge
Deux témoins à décharge
Les jurés

L'accusé, Monsieur X (one of the class), est accusé de tentative d'homicide par imprudence. Voici l'histoire:

'Monsieur X travaille à Paris. Il habite dans un appartement dans le 16e arrondissement mais tient aussi une résidence secondaire dans le petit village de St Ouen sur Marne à 80 kilomètres au sud de Paris où il passe ses weekends.

'En août 1985 à la suite de plusieurs cambriolages il a employé un détective pour essayer de trouver par quel moyen le voleur est arrivé à entrer dans sa maison pendant la semaine, malgré un signal d'alarme, sans toucher aux verrous.

'Le détective a constaté que le cambrioleur était entré par la cheminée et a conseillé à Monsieur X de la boucher. Monsieur X a demandé au détective si, en fermant la cheminée en bas, il risquait de coincer le voleur si celui-ci tentait de nouveau d'entrer dans sa maison. Le détective a répondu à l'affirmatif et lui a conseillé de fermer la cheminée près du toit.

'Il paraît que Monsieur X a ignoré ses conseils et a entrepris les travaux lui-même pour boucher la cheminée à sa base. (Il a insisté devant le juge d'instruction que c'était plus facile.) Il a terminé les travaux le weekend du 6 septembre et il est retourné à Paris ''tranquille''.

'En retournant à St Ouen le weekend suivant il a été horrifié de trouver un petit garçon de 10 ans, Gaston, dans la cheminée, le bras cassé, et inconscient. Il était là depuis trois jours et est encore à l'hôpital. (Change the dates if necessary.)

'Et voilà Monsieur X aujourd'hui devant la Cour d'Assise, accusé de tentative d'homicide par imprudence.'

This simulation will take longer than previous ones both to set up and to perform. The actual trial should be recorded on cassette, or even better on video. (Like all trials, it makes compulsive television.) As well as the judge, prosecutor and defence counsel there are the following witnesses for the prosecution (les témoins à charge):

1 Le détective
2 Un voisin, dont le chien a été la première victime du 'sadisme' de Monsieur X. Le chien s'était égaré dans son jardin et Monsieur X n'a pas hésité à lui tirer dessus.
3 La mère de Gaston.

The witnesses for the defence (les témoins à décharge) are as follows:

1 Une voisine, veuve avec deux enfants de 5 et 7 ans, qui trouve incompréhensible que Monsieur X ait voulu piéger exprès le pauvre petit Gaston. Au contraire, Monsieur X aime les enfants et permet aux siens de jouer dans son jardin même quand il n'est pas là.
2 Un collègue, qui travaille avec lui depuis quinze ans et qui trouve que Monsieur X est un homme sympathique, sérieux et correct.
3 Monsieur X lui-même, qui insiste que la seule raison pour laquelle il a bouché la cheminée en bas, est parce que c'était à la fois plus pratique et moins cher.

There are therefore nine roles. You may want to invent further witnesses, a journalist to write notes for a newspaper article. For a very large class those who do not have roles could be the jury.

For a smaller class where everyone has a role when, after the *plaidoyers* and summing up, everyone except the judge and the accused could become the jury and, based solely on what happened in the trial, come to a verdict. Excluding the judge and defendant from these proceedings adds to the drama at the end when the verdict is announced!

In all roles the students use their own names and where possible they should take a role that corresponds to the extent to which they are sympathetic or not to the defendant's predicament.

For next time

1 Activités

2 A l'écoute

3 Give them a photocopy of Figure 11 in **France Extra!** and ask them to find out as much as possible about what the various dishes are.

11 Tradition et gastronomie

Describing menu items
Saying how dishes are cooked

Structures and exponents:

. . . c'est quoi, exactement?
Pourriez-vous me dire ce que c'est que . . .?

C'est ce qu'on appelle . . .

C'est	un plat	qui est	composé(e) de . . .
	un dessert		fait(e) avec . . .
	une sauce		un mélange de . . .
			une sorte de . . .
			d'origine . . .

The passive form	used in phrases
The reflexive form	

such as:

le vin se boit chambré
le plat se sert chaud
   est servi

To be revised: Language of ordering in a restaurant and simple
descriptions of food
A vous la France! Chapter 7

Tips

1 Start by going through **Pour en savoir plus** I. Practise thoroughly
the tricky pronunciation of phrases with *ce que* in them, such
as '*Pourriez-vous me dire ce que c'est . . .?*' and '*C'est ce qu'on
appelle . . .*'

2 In pairs: **Essayez donc!**

3 *Jigsaw listening*: Dialogues I and 4. Give every student the
following list of questions:
Un dîner chez Monsieur Combourieu

L'hors d'oeuvre
1 List the ingredients of le *pounti*.
2 How is it cooked?
3 How has Auvergnat cooking evolved in recent years?

Le plat principal
4 Where does Monsieur Combourieu get his salmon trout? Why doesn't he use bass? Who is Paul Bocuse?
5 Why won't Monsieur Combourieu tell Nicole how to make *la Sauce Choron*?

La truffade
6 List the ingredients of *la truffade*.
7 How has its preparation evolved?

Le dessert
8 What goes into *le nègre en chemise*?
9 What has Monsieur Combourieu against today's *crème chantilly*?
10 What is the special characteristic of *la cuisine auvergnate*?

4 Group 1 should take Dialogue 1 and answer questions 1 to 3.
Group 2 will work with Dialogues 2 and 3 and answer questions 4 to 7.
Group 3 will work with Dialogue 4 and answer questions 8 to 10.

5 Go through **Pour en savoir plus** 2 and **Essayez donc!**

6 In groups of four have them go through *Figure 11* in **France Extra!** describing the dishes that they know to each other. Re-mix the groups so that everyone's knowledge is shared. This will generate lots of practice of the phrases learnt in **Pour en savoir plus** 1 and the use of the reflexive and the passive described in **Pour en savoir plus** 2. End the activity by describing the dishes on the menu that none of the class has heard of (you may need to have done some homework yourself!).

7 In pairs: **Activité** 1.

Ideas
1 Proceed as in the practical session described in Unit 5 (page 33) but this time have them working in pairs from the *recette* which forms **Activité** 2.

2 If there is a French restaurant in your town organise a dinner with your group. With a little luck the proprietor may be French and be prepared to answer questions in French. Contact him and ask in advance. He may even be prepared to bring his menu to the class and explain some of the dishes!
   If you live in the South of England a day trip to France incorporating lunch at a restaurant in Dunkerque, Calais or Boulogne will probably work out only a little more expensive and would be a marvellous occasion.

For next time
1 A l'écoute

2 On a piece of paper draw a plan of your house or flat.

12 Le troisième âge

Structures and exponent:

avoir tendance à + infinitive
avoir un côté   + infinitive

Quantifiers:

un peu
plutôt
vraiment
extrêmement

Vocabulary of personality description
Vocabulary of the home

Faire + infinitive

To be revised: Order and agreement of adjectives
A vous la France! p. 82

Tips

1   *La parole aux retraités!* The chances are that you will have at least
three or four retired people in your class. Break the class into the
same number of groups as there are retired people, put one retired
person in each group and ask the others in the group to find out (in
French) as much as they can about the person's lifestyle.
   One (non-retired!) person in each group will then report back
to the others on what they have found out.

2   *Listening* – Dialogue 1. Pre-questions:
  1   What does Madame Darris enjoy doing? Where does Monsieur
     Darris spend a lot of his time?
  2   What is her attitude to her 'little aches and pains'?
  3   What is her advice to retired people?

Play the cassette, check answers to the pre-questions, then ask the
question: *'Comment décrivez-vous le caractère de Madame Darris?'*
(*gai, optimiste, sociable, affectueux, épanoui, chaleureux* . . .)

3 Go through **Pour en savoir plus** I and refer the students to the list of adjectives in **Pour en savoir plus**. Ask them to copy down (a) the adjectives which apply to them, (b) those which apply to their husband, wife, boyfriend, girlfriend or best friend. Put them in pairs and have them first compare their lists. Encourage them to ask each other questions; having a list of adjectives which applies to their absent other half gives them the choice as to how personal they become in their questions. Let them decide. Depending on your relationship with your class you may ask them to describe your personality.

4 In pairs: Give them a photo of someone they don't know and ask them to imagine that person's personality. Introduce the exponents *'il/elle a l'air . . .' and 'je dirais qu'il/elle est plutôt . . .'*. In both activities 3 and 4 encourage them to use phrases such as:

j'ai	tendance à . . .
elle a	un côté . . .
il a	un . . . caractère
	une personnalité assez . . .

The home – Take the students through **Pour en savoir plus** 2 and **Le mot juste**. They will find these sections very valuable. Do the **Essayez donc!** exercises too.

5 Having already drawn a plan of their house or flat, ask them in groups of three (a) to describe their homes to each other, and (b) any plans they have for *bricolage* as well as things they have already changed or had changed. If they do have plans to change things around in their house, encourage them to ask advice from the others in the groups. Feed them the structure *Tu pourrais . . . Vous pourriez . . .* Give them a chance to report back on their conversation to the rest of the class as they wish.

6 In pairs: **Activités** I and 2.

Ideas
1 In groups of four: A mini-simulation. You have two million francs. Design an ideal house, within that budget, that the four of you would be willing to share. Take into account personalities and tastes!

Each group then presents their designs to the others.

2 A *Say what you want session* should prove interesting at this point.

For next time
1 Write a descriptive paragraph to accompany the plan you have made of your home.

2 Faits divers.

3 **Activités** 3 and 4.

13 Le sport au pays basque

Structures and exponents:

Je me sens . . .

Adjectives to describe feelings
Past participles used as adjectives

que, qui
ce qui, ce qui

J'ai été (étonné)   v.   J'étais (énervé)
J'ai eu (peur)   J'avais (peur)

manquer

Qu'est-ce que tu ressens/vous ressentez?

Comment | tu te sens?
        | vous sentez-vous?

Tips

1   From the list of adjectives under **Pour en savoir plus** I, try and get
    hold of some photographs or magazine pictures of people
    expressing as many of the feelings described as possible. You may
    need to draw the most obvious ones yourself. (As the students will
    be speculating on the feeling expressed they don't have to be very
    good.)
        Give them a list of the adjectives without the English translation
    and ask them in pairs to go through the list, discuss their meaning
    and look up in a dictionary (Larousse *Dictionnaire du français
    langue étrangère* would be ideal) those they either don't know or
    aren't sure of.
        Distribute the pictures to the pairs and ask them, again using
    '*Il/elle a l'air* . . .' or '*je dirais qu'il/elle est plutôt* . . .', what they
    think the person in the picture is feeling. Make sure the pictures
    are circulated so that all the pairs have seen most of them.
        Collect in the pictures and choose three or four of the less
    obvious ones to show to the reassembled class and see how many
    adjectives for the same picture are suggested (*ravi, content, heureux,
    soulagé, surpris étonné, sidéré, énervé, irrité, fâché, furieux*, etc).

2 Listening – Dialogue 3 up to '. . . *c'est le cri de joie*.' Find out if there are any '*sportifs*' in the class. Ask them (in French) if they get very excited when they play. How do they feel when they win? How do they feel when they lose? Use phrases such as '*Comment tu te sens?*' and '*Qu'est-ce que vous ressentez?*', then write them up.

Then ask the group to name some of the sports played in France: *le foot, le rugby, le tennis, les courses de chevaux, les boules, la pétanque, le cyclisme et la pelote* – Refer them to the introductory paragraph and give them time to read it (up to: '. . . *mais aussi d'instruments.*') Answer questions about it with particular regard to the pronunciation of new words.

Introduce Fanfan, *joueur de pelote* and tell them that Ermi is interviewing him just after '*une partie de pelote*'. It is also worth telling them in advance of Fanfan's strong accent and rapid speech. Play just the first sentence of Dialogue 3 up to '. . . *une bonne partie*' with the pre-question '*Pensez-vous qu'il a gagné la partie?*'

In view of their undoubted difficulty in understanding Fanfan, continue to play the dialogue in snippets with a suitable pre-question or explanation.

For the next part, up to '. . . *la réussite sans confiance*', pre-teach *prendre l'ascendant* (to get on top), *remonter* (to pull back), *la confiance, la réussite*.

Explain that for the third part (from the beginning of Ermi's second question to '. . . *c'est pas le cri nerveux, c'est, le cri de joie*'), Ermi is trying to find out what he's shouting – '*Est-ce qu'il est énervé ou est-ce que ce sont des cris de joie?*'

Stop at the end of that section and then play the three parts together without stopping.

3 Go through **Pour en savoir plus** 2 – practise *que, qui, ce que, ce qui*. Have them do the **Essayez donc!** exercises in pairs.

4 The **Le mot juste** section is again very interesting, particularly the part which deals with *manquer*.

Ideas

Le Jeu des adjectifs – One person goes out of the room and the group thinks of an adjective of feeling, for example *fâché*. The person them comes back in and in order to guess the word asks various people to do particular things, like opening a window or tying a shoelace, in the mood of the feeling described.

A more demanding form of the same game is to have two people guessing two different adjectives that the group have allotted to them at the same time, so that when acting out the tasks asked of them everyone has to remember which of the two people is trying to guess which word. (The two guessers take turns in asking people to do things.)

For next time

1 Activités
2 Listen to Dialogues I and 2 with René and Jean-Michel and follow the texts to get used to their accent. Do the **Avez-vous bien compris?** exercises.

14 Vie culturelle, animation locale

Talking about your interests and tastes
Listening to broadcast announcements
Understanding weather forecasts

Structures and exponents:

s'intéresser à quelque chose
intéresser quelqu'un
être intéressé par quelque chose

Numbers and figures used in public information

To be revised: Numbers

Everyday words for the weather

Il fait	beau	il pleut
	mauvais	il neige
	chaud	
	froid	
	du soleil	
	gris	
	nuageux	

Tips

1 Bring in a 'What's on in Paris' magazine such as *Pariscope* or
L'Officiel du Spectacle or, alternatively use the pages of a Paris-
based newspaper which covers *les Arts et le Spectacle*. Photocopy
the cinema pages and ask them in groups of three to answer the
following questions:
1 What are the different categories of film (for example, *drame
psychologique, film d'horreur*)?
2 What do *VO* and *VF* mean?
3 What does *en première exclusivité* mean?
4 * What does *relâche le dimanche* mean?
5 * Why is Monday a good day to go to the cinema? (The seats are
cheaper.)

2 Go through the answers and write up all the different types of film
which come up, plus those not mentioned by the students.
Go through **Pour en savoir plus** 1.
* Where applicable   Do **Essayez donc!** in pairs.

58

Photocopy and give out the following questionnaire:

Nom:

Cinéma
'Je vais au cinéma souvent/parfois/très peu'
Quelle est votre attitude envers les catégories de film
ci-dessous?

Le film comique
Le documentaire
Le drame psychologique
Le film d'horreur
Le film d'aventure
La science-fiction (la SF)
La comédie musicale
Le film étranger

Lecture
'Je lis beaucoup/parfois/très peu'
Quelle est votre attitude envers les différents genres
ci-dessous?

Le roman
Le roman policier
La nouvelle
La poésie
La biographie
La bande dessinée

Figure 11

Write the following list of possible answers on the board (or
beforehand on a photocopy):

Ça me passionne (énormément)/Je trouve ça passionnant.		
J'en suis fana		+3 points
Je m'y intéresse	(beaucoup)	+2 points
Ça m'intéresse		
C'est pas mal		+1 point
Bof!		−1 point
Ça ne m'intéresse pas	tellement	
Je ne m'y intéresse pas	beaucoup	−2 points
	du tout	
Ça ne me dit	pas grand'chose	−3 points
	rien (du tout)	

Practise the answers orally and also check that they understand
the meaning of all categories in the questionnaire.

Un sondage – They are going to circulate and fill in as many
questionnaires for each other as possible using questions such as:

Qu'est-ce que vous pensez du
Vous vous intéressez au
Ça vous intéresse, le | film d'horreur?
Ça vous dit quelque chose, le

answering with a number according to the answers they get (thereby reducing the writing to a minimum and speeding up the process).

Give them as many copies of the questionnaire as they need to keep going for, say, 15 minutes and suggest they stand so that they can move easily from one person to the next.

At the end of 15 minutes, stop them and correlate the results on the board, totalling the number of points given in answer to each question to reflect the preferences of the group as a whole.

2   Listening – Dialogue 1, Madame Lambert. Play the dialogue twice (up to '. . . ces pays-là') and ask them in threes to fill in the questionnaire as they think Madame Lambert would. Encourage discussion (and argument!) in French. Play the dialogue (again only up to '. . . ces pays-là) a third time if requested. Ask each group to report back.

3   Public Information – Go through **Pour en savoir plus** 2. Practise addresses and telephone numbers thoroughly. You may feel it necessary to play a couple of games of bingo to revise numbers thoroughly (see page 99, Unit 2).

For the weather forecast terminology photocopy a French newspaper's weather map for extra practice.

4   *Listening* – Radio broadcast. Give out the following questions (in English):

1   You are not sure, this weekend, whether to go for a picnic in the country or to go ski-ing. On the basis of the weather forecast on *Radio 15* what will you do?

2   You are looking for a summer job and you are a good swimmer. What address and telephone number might it be a good idea to contact?

3   As it happens you haven't been for a swim for ages and would love to go to the swimming pool. How long will you have to wait?

4   You also love dogs, particularly poodles, and have been thinking of getting one, but they are so expensive from pet shops. Where might you go instead? What number should you phone? Can you ring in the evening?

Before playing the radio extract pre-teach the following:

un maître nageur
la SPA
un caniche

This is realistic since if the above interests were real they would be looking for these words when listening to the radio.

Ideas

1 Bring is some good *BDs*, for example, *Astérix, Tintin, Claire Bretécher*, etc and lend them out. If their interests in *BD* can be stimulated it will be of considerable benefit to them to go on reading them in the future. *BD* in French *are* available in England through the larger bookshops. At least some of the students are bound to get as hooked as thousands of French adults!

2 *Simulation* – A radio/television local magazine programme. Follow the same procedure as in the simulation *Notre Ville* in Unit 2 (page 20).

 The basis for material should be a French (local) newspaper or *Authentik* (see page 287). Additional roles will be that of the newsreader, weatherman and arts correspondent.

Each 10-minute programme should contain:

The News Headlines
Interviews with people in the news
A review of what's on at the cinema
(optional: a review of a new book)
Tomorrow's weather

3 To practise the alphabet:

 1 Letter Bingo. Write seven letters on each card instead of numbers. Read out letters at random.
 2 Dictate the spelling of an obvious phrase or long word for them to guess.

For next time

1 Read **Le saviez-vous?** on *Les Radio Libres*.

2 **A l'écoute** – more from *Radio 15*.

3 Start getting into the habit of listening to French radio, particularly if you have a radio-cassette machine for recording and referring to. We're coming to the end of the course and radio will be your only source of spoken French for a while, and you can learn a great deal on your own that way.

15 De tout et de rien

Structures and exponents:

Reported speech: il a dit qu'il . . .
  il lui a demandé | si elle . . .
  | ce qu'elle . . .

le mien, le sien, le tien, etc
à moi, à lui, à toi, etc

Je suis | en train de | + infinitive
  | sur le point de |

To be revised: Indirect pronouns: lui, leur, etc

Je viens de + infinitive
France Extra! Chapter 10
Parts of the body
A vous la France! Chapter 9, p. 187

Tips

1 Begin by explaining the meaning of *de tout et de rien* and why this final chapter is so called. They are going to hear from a couple of ladies who have just met the former French President and his former Prime Minister (don't say their names), a couple of women who make cuddly toys, an astrologer, the owner of a splendid veteran car and a well-travelled lady born in the last century.

2 Ask the class if any of them have ever met somebody vaguely famous (if only locally). (In my experience, there is always someone who has a story to tell!) Ask that person to recount in French what he/she said to the celebrity and what the celebrity said to him/her. The student is likely to say such things as '*il m'a dit: "je suis heureux de faire votre connaissance."*' without putting it into reported speech. As the student tells the story write up what was said on the board as below leaving a space between the lines:

Je lui ai dit 'C'est la première fois que je rencontre un homme si célèbre'.

Il m'a dit 'Je suis heureux de faire votre connaissance'.

Et puis il m'a demandé 'Vous venez souvent ici?'

etc

When he/she has finished, ask a few questions about the incident (and allow others to ask questions) and then suggest that there is, as in English, a way of eliminating the use of *je, vous* and inverted commas to make it easier on the ears. This is called reported speech. Then rewrite the above sentences in the space between the lines as follows:

Je lui ai dit que c'était la première fois que je rencontrais un homme si célèbre.

Il m'a dit qu'il était heureux de faire ma connaissance.

Et puis il m'a demandé si j'y venais souvent.

etc

Once you have written a couple of sentences different members of the class may feel able to continue.

3 Go through **Pour en savoir plus** 1a and 1b, including the **Essayez donc!** exercise in pairs.

4 *Listening* – Dialogue 1 Nicole 'Qu'est ce que vous lui avez dit tout à l'heure?' to the end.
   Set the scene by saying that Bernadette and Monique have just met two very famous politicians. Pre-questions:

1   Who are the two politicians?
2   What sport does the ex-President play well?
3   Whom does his daughter resemble.
4   How many times did the ex-Prime Minister speak to them? (He didn't – but he did shake hands with them a few times!)

Pre-teach:
passer le chamois
repérer

Play the cassette once and then again if they want you to in order to answer the questions. Go through their answers.
   Go back to Nicole's question *'Qu'est-ce que vous lui avez dit tout à l'heure?'* Have them repeat the question chorally and then play Bernadette's answer line by line for repetition up to '. . . et il m'a promis son passage'.
   Go through **Pour en savoir plus** 2 (including **Essayez donc!**).

5 *Les jouets en peluche* – They should know most of the names for parts of the human body (revise them if necessary) with the possible exception of *les joues* and *le bout du nez*. They are unlikely, however, to know parts of animals' anatomy such as *les pattes*, *le bec*.

As for the names of the animals, brainstorm the class (in French) for those animals which make good cuddly toys. Write up all the above animals as they come up and add the ones that are not mentioned.

6 *Listening* – Play the whole of Dialogue 2 and ask them to note down the names of all the animals they hear (there are 12 mentioned). Do so twice and get them to try and get all 12 by consulting other members of the class.

Play up to Marie saying '. . . *les petits yeux noirs*'. There are 11 words referring to the anatomy (including the word *le corps*). As before, have them collaborate to get the 11 – it should not be competitive.

Focus, then, on the two questions '*Qu'est-ce que vous êtes en train de faire?*' and '*Qu'êtes-vous en train de faire?*'. Point out also that the word *là* added to the end of a question in the simple present as in '*Qu'est-ce que vous faites là?*' has a similar function to *être en train de faire*, in that it makes clear the idea of 'at this moment' rather than 'in general'. Refer them to **Pour en savoir plus** 3 and **Le mot juste** section referring to *tout à l'heure*.

7 *L'astrologue* – Prepare two lists, one of the birthsigns in French with the corresponding dates (see **Activité** 1 if you don't know them), and one of all the students in the class. Photocopy them, give one copy of each to all of them and go through the pronunciation of all of the signs, repeating chorally.

Ask them to get up and circulate, asking everyone in the class when their birthday is and then noting their sign against their name. Each exchange should go as follows:

'Sam, c'est quand, ton anniversaire?'
'Le 7 avril.:'
'Ah bon. Alors, tu es bélier, n'est-ce pas?'
'C'est ça.'

When everyone has got round the whole class, go through the list of names, asking '*Sue, elle est quel signe?*', etc. If you know a little about astrology yourself, or, even better, if there is an amateur astrologer in the group, this would be a perfect opportunity to revise adjectives of personality first covered in Unit 2. Introduce the reflexive verb *s'entendre* ('*Sue est balance, Sam est bélier. Alors ils ne devraient pas s'entendre. Par contre Sue doit s'entendre bien avec Janet*, etc!').

Ideas
1 Get hold of a real horoscope from a French magazine and photocopy it. Invite comment!

2 A final (sad? personal? emotional?) *Say what you want* session!